# About the Author

H. K. G. Lowery is a Poet from the North East of England. In July 2020, Lowery graduated from Newcastle University with a BA Honours degree in English Literature receiving First Class grades for his Poetry and his essays on Ezra Pound and Immanuel Kant. In his two years of writing, Lowery has composed over 500 poems that span across three collections of Poetry. He has been shortlisted for the Terry Kelly Poetry Prize 2020, and his work has been accepted into many anthologies including Train River Publishing and Sylvia Magazine. Lowery also travels around the United Kingdom playing shows with his band, Fossway.

Poetry Instagram: @_hkglowery_

# Dedication

To Jacob Herrington, for making my time at university memorable.

H. K. G. Lowery

# AN ENQUIRY INTO THE DELIGHT OF EXISTENCE AND THE SUBLIME

AUSTIN MACAULEY PUBLISHERS™

LONDON · CAMBRIDGE · NEW YORK · SHARJAH

A CIP catalogue record for this title is available from the British Library.

ISBN 9781528980135 (Paperback)
ISBN 9781528980159 (ePub e-book)

www.austinmacauley.com

First Published (2020)
Austin Macauley Publishers Ltd
25 Canada Square
Canary Wharf
London
E14 5LQ

# Acknowledgements

This particular collection of Poetry is very close to me and was written following a difficult stage of my life. I would not have been able to overcome that stage of my life or complete this work without the continued support, work and love from those around me.

To my mother and father, I am indebted to you both forever for everything you have done and do for me. I am forever grateful for the love and support you continually give me. Thank you for everything.

To my friends and family, I am truly blessed to be part of such a large and loving family and group of friends. I would like to thank you all for everything you have done for me throughout my life.

Thanks to Professor Bill Herbert of Newcastle University. The assessment of the module 'Poetry Workshop' was to compose a collection of twelve poems. It is a surreal dream come true to see these poems published. I am very grateful for the wisdom-filled seminars that educated me particularly on poetic form and theme.

Thanks to Professor Alex Niven of Newcastle University. Although this collection was composed before my taking of Professor Niven's module 'Pound to the Beats', his lectures on Pound, Bunting and Ginsberg have since expanded my love of Poetry and have since influenced my third collection of poetical work.

Of course, none of this would be possible without the work and professionalism of Austin Macauley. I am eternally grateful for this opportunity, it is a dream fulfilled.

Finally, I must thank Samuel Taylor Coleridge and Percy Bysshe Shelley. Thank you for your work and for trying to make sense of this thing we call life. I am blessed to know your works in my own existence, it is forever inspiring.

# Table of Contents

# Preface

"I have said that poetry is the spontaneous overflow of powerful feelings; it takes its origin from emotions recollected in tranquillity."
William Wordsworth, Preface to 'Lyrical Ballads'.

If you are found to read this, please indulge me to express my innermost indebtedness for your kind support. To hold this collection of poetry in your hands means more to me than my words could ever convey. Thank you ever so much.

It may be of interest to you if I were to take half a moment to provide you with a brief commentary to accompany this collection of poetical work. It will not, however, offer a perusal of each poem as I believe myself to be an avid supporter that any piece of literature should be interpreted by the sole reader alone. Poetry is not absolute, but rather infinite – what it means to the Poet may mean a thousand things different to the reader.

This literary work had seen its birth following a difficult stage of my life that heightened a depression in my life during that time. It unfortunately became an existential matter, for I often found myself falling into the cruel jaws of nihilism. At a challenging time early in my life, I would not know that this same darkness would lead me to what I consider to be the light of my life. From an unhappy time, I had discovered my love and passion for writing, and I find it most evident that these two polarities of despair and delight bleed into one another in my first poetical work (this is indeed my first collection of poetry, and so I do apologise for its incompetence). However, it is in these polarities, the polarities of life and those of myself, where this collection of poetical work finds its place in the literary thematic landscape, which is, of course, so rich yet so barren in recent times. Thereon, from this landscape, this collection achieves its form: it is a journey. It is a journey of self-acceptance, redemption, forgiveness, the search for happiness and meaning, and the translation of existential dread; in the sense I hold both love and dislike for elements of both life and existence.

Of course, an enquiry into the void of existentialism and nihilism would not be so much complete without the role, or acknowledgement, of a God (Please note I do not desire to postulate the figure of God in this or any other of my works, though it is a concept that can be considered and included). For context, I was raised in the Roman Catholic faith, however, around the time of this composition, I believe my faith to have channelled to, though not diminished to, Christianity that is reserved. I do not so much follow, or rather practice, perceived doctrine and the attendant liturgy, but rather my relationship with what or whom I perceive to be God is found to be very intimate and malleable to my own personal struggles, needs and thoughts. Therefore, understanding the concept of there being meaning to this madness, or rather madness to the meaning, this poetical work highlights faith, not so much in the dogmatic context of doctrine, but rather every element of faith for what it is: a struggle. It is indeed a struggle to love something that is omnipotent, omnibenevolent and omniscient but does not seem to interfere with its own creation, which I assume is a common obstacle for those who struggle with faith. It is also a struggle to love something you do not, or perhaps cannot, see or hear. But with these words, faith is indeed faith. It is the ownership of the faith to believe that the trail of crumbs will lead you to immortality and most importantly, the truth of love. Therefore, when faith is drawn upon in this work, it is most often met with fear and uncertainty; a fear from the degree of faith, and uncertainty in myself, in God and in death. And with this said, I, like many, do fall into nihilism, struggling with my faith, and thereon my faith in an afterlife, a purpose and a meaning. I will say that we will all leave this world as clueless as we came, but I am fond to desire I have faith in the concept of an afterlife, and I am fond to desire I have faith that nothing does not mean anything, but rather everything means something. And, therefore, I have faith, or perhaps hope, in my writing that it may help those who read it, with these thoughts and those of their own.

It is these collections of thoughts that form the basis and inspiration for my first literary work. From the personal experience of myself, if everything means something, or even if nothing means anything, I have found some purpose in my life. I have found delight, and thereon purpose, to write poetry and novels, to continue my efforts with Fossway, and above all, to be in the continuous pursuit of happiness and peace. This is where I believe myself to have found the delight of existence, rather than the despair of existence.

One avenue that led me to this thought was the entity of acceptance. Its profound and prominent role that this collection exhibits, highlights its necessity and importance. I have come to accept there is no singular moment in our little lives when we will achieve happiness; the journey of life only brings more, and so very different commitments, anxieties and delights. I have come to accept nothing is guaranteed. And I have come to accept, with innermost difficulty, he of who I am. There is an overarching acceptance of this work, that we live and then we die. However, it is between these two polarities where the beauty, or rather delight, of life itself resides, for what is beauty without pain? Therefore, if nothing so dreadfully means anything, our sole purpose as homo sapiens must be love and kindness in ourselves and to one another, until death sweeps away everything we have ever become. This collection is indeed an enquiry into this matter. Our world is sadly full of hurt, but it is in the little years of our little lives whereby we must populate the air we breathe with happiness, kindness and gentleness. We may never set the world free from hatred, but we may set our minds free from it.

From the despair to the delight, at the climax of cathartic outpour of this poetical work, I believe myself to continuously grow towards and closer to reason, to purpose and to meaning. It is by manic and obsessive efforts I attempt to find reason behind this thing we call life, and the final poem of my collection reflects and concludes this search and stance: I believe life to be the satisfaction of death. Everything we do now is so that we are satisfied at the hour of our death. My only desire from this poetical work was to be as honest in myself and in my writing as possible.

On this truly jovial note, I very much hope life is kind to you, and once again, I would like to express my most sincere gratitude for your kind support.

May you enjoy this collection as much as I did composing it.


Love always,

H. K. G. Lowery

# An Ode to Father John Misty

*The sky is sewn with stars and a mystery, through Nature or nurture, how we have come to be,*

Drink with me now.

We can be famous to ourselves
when nothing else matters.

This century, the paper republic from torn wings looks
down on Syrian soil
and the rainbow they bleach.

A civil union upon an altar and the Father's absence.
With no pride, a lion sleeps amid the wild
without his lioness;
but these mammals dread Nature.

Fear. The content in people I see
kindly killing their hours as they wonder
what repast teeth will gnaw
if you dive into his eyes, you'll see plans of suicide.
I bet he'd do anything for sex and cigarettes.

Hello friend, I find you armed in apparel,
branded by brands. Moths
drawn to the likes and views –
I kiss my teeth to you all.
And you can wear a Beatles T-shirt, just tell me your favourite song – mine is
*Helter Skelter*.

Click,
and add this to your basket,
start your free trial online today, K?
So please be kind, donate,
and for just nine-nighty-nine a month
you can stop the ice that slips away from
under the paws of a polar bear and her poor offspring.

That thing religion -

the group of beggars arguing with each other where the piece of bread lies. How many lives hang
on the nuance of a single word
as they obey the words fed to them from the lizards in suits.
The millions are not woke.
In seven weeks it will be fashionable to believe in God again and one day we might see a woman in a white collar
preaching to the girls and boys in the pews.

So take me to the depths of the afternoon,
away from varsity, that sober tournament.
I am bruised—a grain of salt.
Alas! They are but the kings that wear no clothes.

After dinner and the dishes,
it will be time to carve the next number into my prison wall,
moving around the city, describing my life to taxi drivers
as fingering despair.
                    Sorrow is the new romance.

         "This human experiment will reach its violent end
         but I look at you
         as our second drinks arrive
         the piano player's playing 'This Must Be the Place'
         and it's a miracle to be alive"

We are the mindless monkeys roaming around in this infinite cage,
fixed on screens, where the treadmills of thumbs
numbs each and every soul
where men are not measured by meaning.
Ladies, this is the survival of the shittest.

We'll be underground when this is all over,
when the historians find us,
the frozen pixels of the digital zoo,
the miracle-turned tragedy.

And as the clock from twenty-three fifty-nine turns to

zero,
         zero,
                  zero,
                           zero —

drink with me now and
do not expect applause.

# In Limbo I

*I was lost, depressed by hourly moments,*

I am suspended between two nowheres;

between the nowhere of intellect

between the nowhere of careless hedonism

nowhere, where two paths cease

harmony.

I am falling

but I do not know from          what or through.

In being between two nowheres,

I am nowhere,

I am the nowhere.

Where no soul knows where it is,

I am          conjured and do not belong.

The theory of nowhere is fear.

Though the language of my pillow          is not yet extinct.

# The Ballad of a Philophobic

*abandoned into isolation with Hope; Love's orphan.*

Is fate a fantasy, or fantasy a fate?
A day I would fall in love to a day
I now fall from love. My crucible,
hosted past; to stimulate memory
of what has gone before me, from somewhere
so far, yet so close—
a million memories
held at hostage
as they forego their dying presence;
fading before me
prophetic to Time's will.
And as my mind chronicles everything:
it haunts me, it haunts me, it haunts me.

A midnight of panic,
I dwell with deep thought: what a mind can summon,
as drunken with disorder, I will say:
love is a context. With lavish lament
cold are the unwelcome clouds
where under sleep hidden secrets
known to no other ear but my own –
there is all so much grief where sorrow is fair.
This terror sits behind my eyes
like an unremembered dream,
so wild and wasted.
Playing each other's
heart strings, hoping to hear same melody.
I still have never heard such a beautiful melody.
It is all conditional. My limbs of lead,
I am callous to survive the cold.
How I have lost one
to another—my blood is cold. Now
I will not be as I have been as I see
but the absence of another dawn;
though no curse prayed for, I do not want to hate.
Say not in grief's whisper we bind no more
but in God's keeping I seek so much to console
as to be consoled. This may not be Hell,

but in perturbed reason my demons drag themselves
down from Damn, I am exiled to Lucy.
Kissed by sorrow, I lay on fire,
I dance in the flames, I smile in the wildfire;
there is nothing of love my heart tames:
it harms me, it harms me, it harms me.

To suffer on the sands of sorrow,
I am on the shore
where dreams trouble my waking life,
where ghosts breathe the disease
that is despair
into this chamber, between four walls,
I lay in the palm of darkness.
No safety, no surprise—this is the end.
O Holy Hell, desperate am I
for the shoulder of a stranger.
It is so easy to say: 'Fuck the World'
when I hear the memories that haunt these walls
as they echo into my eyes and dance their last dance.
Lust ripped from arterial blood;
I learn to forget with idle regret
how I will never look into your eyes again.
Prisoner of the moment with belief
to be the only metric to matter,
I have dug to my bedrock.
Crowned and crucified,
I am the dying ember of a furious fire once lit.
Once, fantasy was to be my fate,
lest now it be fate that is my fantasy.
They say the pain teaches us
who we are. So I wonder:

was the pain justified?

# Desponysus

*I retreated into my own imagination with a vision unbound,*

With crass gesture, truth seems to hide its candour;
conflicted to applause the fact,
no cadence of rapture,
we ride into perfect oblivion
and the mystery is maintained.
La Spezia struck a storm, slave to fate,
elder tides and the younger
of rocks and sky did collide,
and with screams submerged,
silence returned.
His body lay in sleep on a shore in Lerici
as the hours divided the night to day,
the black mass was held around the pyre,
and what the dying embers did reveal
was a heart unburnt from the flames of the fire.
From ash came a heart centring bone,
wrapped by her in the pages of his final poem;
this is history in her finest hour.
Of what flesh may have died in fire,
a marble legacy left to I to inspire.

*

Of all forms of love, of suffering and of madness;
he searched for himself with hurt gait,
between the first and dying hour,
exhausting the darkest avenue within,
to find all he was and all he was ever to be—
the Poet is the Walker of Water.
He ran with time, not out of it,
a Dionysian of freedom and voice
that unlocks the universal mind
of history in time and universe in space,
weaving an intellectual tapestry amongst all,
that blurs the borders between reality
which dreams beget.
Through canon of good measure,
they seek to find their position

within the cultural pantheon
that art tries to represent,
that science tries to explain.
And lest I settle,
to rival the real,
to reveal the real:
we are nothing,
but we are also everything.

# Sad!

*I began dreaming of what my hands did not hold, what my ears did not hear and what my eyes did not see -*

I have dreams of the night sky full of stars over a lake midnight blue, travelling European cities fleeing from you; I have dreams of songs softly sung, I still ache to know the foreign tongue; I have dreams of a campfire in forest wood, the sparks rise to the sky, and I would follow them if I could; I have dreams of terming freedom like a Saracen, who am I to dream of comparison?; I have dreams of escaping urban sprawls, and retreating to distant land that knows no walls; I have dreams of finding a path to follow again, to translate vocation with the pen; I have dreams of the night we met, and all the memories I try to forget; I have dreams of sitting in the back of the car, watching the rain fall like a cry from afar; I have dreams of being chased, I wonder if anyone remembers what it is to be chaste; I have dreams of fulfilling pride in my mother and father, to be a good son and a good scholar; I have dreams of a world where hate does not spawn so much as the sun in its dawn; I have dreams of being complete, amongst other being able to compete; I have dreams of understanding life, someday I may have children and a wife; I have dreams of being in the lands of Tolkien, with human eyes this sight is seldom seen; I have dreams of fine celebrations with Mr Mercury and my friend Jay, I never remember what his drunk lips say; I have dreams of writing like one of the greats, on my dying day seek reassurance in pearly gates; I have dreams of sitting with Samuel eating Opium bars, we laugh at the barracudas as they swim into the stars; I have dreams of meeting Plato in a place far from here, he tells me the tales of what it is to be a seer; I have dreams of standing in the presence of Percy, he tells me tales of love and mercy; I have dreams of talking to John, Matthew, Mark and Paul, and the keys to the meaning of it all; and I have dreams of nothing

# In Limbo II

*what I was anxious to define; call it fear,*

I met you when I was fourteen,   and that's strange because fourteen is my lucky number since then you still have never shown your face     nor do I know you have one you follow my body as it moves from place    to place I cannot rid you I do not like talking about you    and I'm sure the others do not one day you bled into my blood the red black became a part of me but this is my body it is not your body you do not let me smile you make each day feel like an extra mile to my credits who are you    and why won't you leave    you're hurting me my shadow my shadow my shadow     my shadow when I look in the mirror I do not see myself you take the teeth away from a tiger and what is he then

# The Silas Tomkyn Comberbache Club

*I learnt to carry it, running with my collective.*

I had not seen seven summers
when mine ear met the Mariner,
before somewhere,
      far from urban veins,
      far from concrete chains,
spoke to me,
amongst sun, sea
and the sky that held no moon
on that day months from May and June
that autumn leaves, hues of orange,
did conquer; from a threshold came a cellar door
hinged by the sense to belong.
I became closer by the inch.
In the sight of darkness, the choice to dare,
in the lungs of solitude there was a prayer
that discoursed realisation:
I take my place with these men of the pen.
Still to this day does it follow
me in my trails,
when the butterflies in my belly
fly on thought of him,
Percy, George and John the same,
their minds like rivers of dreams of delight
that guide me closer to the space
      between the beauty and the pain,
when a discovery was made: there is no best, but a better
I began to champion my place in salt,
alleviating the weight in my heart
in the knowledge there can be
any character inside the nucleus of genius;
how the saints of most importance to the language and its legacy
were not so strict in construct or act,
but rather free in their minds and matters.
Still with this same membership to the pact,
in parallels, I have found happiness and responsibility in and to my relations
heart to heart, closer to the balance with fascination
in its calling, though I cease to submit into delusion.

I obsess to impress humbly
those of whom I was made,
living for myself first, not a selfish but required act
for the inherited search for greater truth yields only
momentary feeding of the hunger—
       to wonder if reason could ever capture the Sublime,
because all we may have is each other,
but with these men of the pen,
that doth seem so kindly fair.
And on that day,   I believe to have taken my place
where my own chronicles begun.

# A Requiem for St. Francis

*How from chaos came the arms of safety,*

**I.**

What deity carves our paths
from the first breath to the last,
crafts every smile shared, hand held and tear torn,
every minute, moment and memory
  under eyes;

with chance and choice, the brothers of our being,
we are able to befriend the stranger who lives amongst us under skin:

to embrace what emotion unfolds like the changing of the seasons,
to welcome the whispers that travel through to where the pines grow,
and to walk with our God,
both through the tempest
and the calm seas that never made great sailors.

**II.**

What creed
of servants and serpents
sends us to Eden soil,
stains our souls
and burns the bowers of our bodies
where flowers weep and birds do not sing
as fear rushes through blood.
  The omnipotence, the benevolence;
do we tear the Shroud of Turin?

In this God-given gift,
render me a new soul alive to live.

Offer your hand for Hope to finesse,
speak in tongues and find your way,
I say what is unsolved should be left
to remain amid the veins of consecration.

More do I subscribe to the premise of the spirit

for what is organised is a casino of beliefs;
an obstacle to what is true faith,
to perceive truly what sacred texts divine.

    In liminal twilight:
    does my voice reach the ears, my troubles to the eyes?
    In which of my doings am I deserved?
    Will I be caught in the arms of safety when I fall?
    The day that is my last, will my leave be taken satisfied?

        What if there is not a haven of our Heaven
    but if Heaven were a state of mind that we so much rarely visit;
            can it be as real as life?

No more do I desire to cease upon sorrow,
but rather see the truth in its numinous and nakedness:
love is liberty.

The hidden blueprint of destiny
where with programmed architecture,
fate arrives the same;
        I will go where I am destined after the last breath.

**III.**

I am at sea with you.

It humbles my heart,
for you are my Hallelujah.

# @ Scargo Lake

*I closed the cellar door*

In the seventh hour
at the mouth of the small pier,
a loud silence
haunts the still air,
wind on water,
it whispers around me,
surfacing the stream
upon the sand of which it rests;
it lays still at my surround,
the goldfinch arrives to drink,
the ripples cannot beat the gentle tranquil;
here in naked existence,
all hath made peace -

an eloquence to the colour and shape,
how the air could collapse any moment
now as the seconds fall,
my Spring was cruel though my Summer kinder;
by my side a steadfast copse takes its place,
branches over my body,
as they unite together
around Scargo lake,
      where all sound has been stolen,
      where all thought has been taken,
      where, in one moment,

        my soul was free.

# In Limbo III

*and as Time turned scars from hurt,*

An ocean.

A
long lost city,
where pillars, turned    grey
from white, stand crumbled
with the ancient language carved
into the skin of stone
from a realm forever ago.

From under decayed stone
lies    a chest, generous in riches,
something no man did find.

Where fierce battles were once held
for a throne;
that a king, untaught,
would take his place upon.

A plateau any marine specie
now uses to swim in the ancient air
beneath the sapient nocturne of Pisces.

      No longer can I see what lies within.

As soft beams of light
pierce gently the moana's might
to a seabed where statues sleep
calm in the midnight weep.

Tell me black ocean,
               am I a good man?

# (46.6863° N, 7.8632 ° E)

*I discovered forgiveness is a journey,*

The way they leave tells you everything.

The land carves itself round
        into its own place. It is not greedy in its taking.

Miles from me now, the same summit still stands.
        A small town sleeps North;
            though through in days coming it is not much more
                alive than its sleep.

Decades, rich in time, spend their viewing
      from the shoulders of the mountains that kiss the sky,
           as the snow is in slumber at the peak.

Spring casts tears upon them that do not dry
      as they become lost, falling
        in the land's depression, gathering and gliding
        around the village they frame so fairly.

The absence of clouds
      sees the sky's atlas, where birds with best eye
      patrol the town; their eyes
        once saw my climb, my ascension of the incline
        with the weight upon my bearing blades.

I remember Nature was honest in her works and her quiet loquacity,
      wonder danced before my eyes in splendour,
        for I had not seen another place to emulate such
        stamina of grandeur.

I was brought to my Autumn.
                    Bronze leaves return to their sombre slumber.


                I dwelled: what is my design?
                            It does not expire to weigh upon the bones of my body,

        but better is it I spent just three days there
                            than make commonplace of its excellence.


If my body were to turn to dust in this
                    moment, I would not be taken so sad,
                            nor be upset in character.


                Hours brought me to mountain's peak,

                        I cut free the weight I for so long carried;


                The way they left told me everything.


I cannot let forgiveness sleep further,
I cannot forfeit love to pride.

            In my submission to the senses,
            I must reconcile what cannot be annulled,
        what roars in the melodies of Justin Vernon.
                    An enemy deceases only after the one within.


                    I have found

                    a paradise

                    of this world.

# Re: Comme Tu Es Belle
# (A Love Letter to the Human Race)

*and I chose to be.*

### I.

The birds have left their trees,
he calls out for something on his knees.

### 11.

The sky is sewn with stars
and a mystery through Nature or nurture
how we have come to be -
I was lost, depressed by hourly moments,
abandoned into isolation with Hope; Love's orphan.
I retreated into my own imagination with a vision unbound,
I began dreaming of what my hands did not hold,
what my ears did not hear and what my eyes did not see—
what I was anxious to define; call it fear,
I learnt to carry it, running with my collective.
How from chaos came the arms of safety,
I closed the cellar door
as Time turned scars from hurt,
I discovered forgiveness is a journey,
and I chose to be.

### III.

If there were to be no purpose
of everything within life,
if ourselves and our actions are not remembered,
then the meaning of life must be
for the satisfaction of death.

And therefore,
there is so much more I have to express in art,
for what is beauty without pain?

In humble affection,
I still search for who I merit my gratitude to,
Nature or nurture,
but one has by good effort not done so bad:


The Delight of Existence and the Sublime
compensate truly for the Despair of Existence in Time.


Yours forever,


*The End*